Pasghetti and Meat Bulbs!

by
BIL KEANE

FAWCETT GOLD MEDAL • NEW YORK

PASGHETTI AND MEAT BULBS!

Published by special arrangement with The Register & Tribune Syndicate, Inc., by Fawcett Gold Medal Books, a unit of CBS Publications, the Consumer Publishing Division of CBS Inc.

ISBN: 0-449-14440-2

Printed in the United States of America

First Fawcett Gold Medal printing: November 1981

10 9 8 7 6 5 4 3 2 1

"This is butter and this is Marjorie."

"What flavor is this, Mommy? Miss Helen said
we're to keep our drawings in a
vanilla folder."

"Dolly's teachin' us our ABZs."

"You're the daddy and I'm the mommy."

"Okay. You take the kids shoppin' and I'll
watch TV."

"Dolly's kissin' Kittycat on the mouth! Will that hurt Kittycat?"

"This is Indian summer."
"Why don't they have it at the same time as everybody else?"

"Why do you have to CLEAN the fish? They couldn't get dirty in the water."

"I don't care what the six million dollar man
likes — the sixty-five cent boy
is going to eat it."

"Dinner's ready." "Ten four."

"Why doesn't Mommy want to be in the picture?"

"Is three rows of cookies for 89 cents a good deal?"

"Want me to put the handles on those little hot dogs?"

"Hi, Mommy! I didn't want to bother you."

"Slower, Daddy. I can't listen that fast."

"You talk to your plants, so I'm readin' a cow-
boy story to my cactus."

"Daddy has to do it because this place doesn't have waiters."

"Mommy won't be off the phone for a long while — she just changed ears."

"Doesn't Daddy have any friends his own age around here to play with?"

"How do you keep so much water in that little hydrant?"

"Want a piggy on your shirt, Daddy?"

"No, I haven't told Daddy yet. Let's let him
enjoy dinner first."

"What are you drawing?"
"I don't know. It isn't finished yet."

"Daddy's switching the wheels around so they all have a chance to ride up front."

"This is a new girl in our school."

"I'm not new — I'm FIVE years old!"

"Daddy, will you turn the TV to 6 o'clock?"

"Mommy! Guess who's using your coffee mug again!"

"I couldn't find any clean towels, so I put out
the ones that say 'Merry Christmas.' "

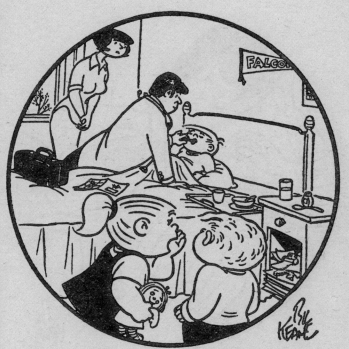

"Maybe Billy will have to go into the shop."

"But, I don't WANT to get better!"

"But, I'm not too sick to watch television. I'm
just too sick to go to school!"

"Why can't we go in? Poor Billy needs a little symphony."

"I'm beginnin' to feel better now, Mommy!
Can I get up?"

"You forgot to write a note 'cause I was absent!"

"I hope none of the other children come down
with the bug Billy had."

"Daddy put those caps on there to keep the
'lectricity from leaking."

"Mommy, will you tell PJ to stop following me around?"

"Daddy, this movie isn't rated 'R' or 'X,'
is it?"

"For cryin' out loud! The year 1955 is in this
HISTORY book!"

"I'm never wearin' this shirt to school again! I
got called on five times today!"

"How good are you at creating droid cos-
tumes? Billy wants to dress up as See-threepio,
Jeffy wants to be Artoo-Detoo . . ."

"Then, when I'd get my allowance, I'd hurry to the Five-and-Ten and . . ."
"What's a 'Five-and-Ten,' Grandma?"

"If trees were people, they'd get a ticket for littering."

"Here, Daddy. It's your ticket for dinner."

"I met Billy's teacher today. She was surprised
I'm not prematurely gray."

"When they do something naughty, that man
makes them back up."

"Turkeys don't come from the zoo, do they?"

"I'm ready to be thankful again, Mommy. Is there any turkey left?"

"Lenny's ready to go home now. We'll be in the car."

"We're going to try to get the goldfish back."

"Let's have halftime now. I'm hungry."

"Who finger painted the windows, Mommy?"

"Before you come in, Mommy — I didn't do it!"

"Do I hafta wash the jelly off my face and hands or can I just let it wear off?"

"Turn that book upside right, PJ, or you'll ruin your eyes."

"Who won the fight?"
"I don't know. I left in the middle of it."

"What'll it be this morning? Porridge, curds and whey or corn flakes?"

"There's somebody under my bed!"

"Planned Parenthood? That means you get to
pick out your mother and father."

"Bein' a grandmother is easier than bein' a
mother 'cause you get more time off."

"Will you buy me a bottle of boat, Mommy?"

"Dolly says I'm the opposite sex and I say she
is. Who's right?"

"Who turned the dark on me?"

"If it comes unassembled, I don't want it."

"Everybody has to put a sweater on. Mommy feels chilly."

"These are the emergency numbers — police,
fire, doctor, Santa Claus . . ."

"Mommy, do reindeer have wings?"

"'Should I say, 'Dear Santa,' or 'Dear Mr. Claus'?"

"We can't play now. We hafta help our daddy
put up the Christmas lights."

"I thought Santa's helpers were ELVES."

"Daddy, will you make a copy of my letter to
Santa so I can send it to Grandma?"

"How can you see into our house from up at
the North Pole?"

"Christmastime is WHISPERtime!"

"Looks like Joan and Bud . . . or Jean and Burl . . . or is that Jim and Bill?"

"I'm going to ask for some things now. Do you
want to get a paper and pencil?"

"Can't I wait a couple days to see if any of the other guys are bringin' presents to Miss Johnson?"

"It's the Walkers' annual newsletter, but I
think I'll wait for the movie."

"If it was a pear tree, there'd be a partridge
in it."

"Jeffy didn't put his tinsel on one at a time!"

"When they're finished singin', do we just smile or clap or what?"

"Hooray! 'Twas the Night Before Christmas'
finally got here!"

"Look what Santa left me and I didn't even
ASK for it! He just KNEW I wanted it!"

"Thank you, Grandma. This is the same game
Santa brought us."

"Why do we hafta thank Aunt Nancy for the robot? We already broke it."

"I'll be the starter. On your mark . . . Ready . . . Get set . . ."

"There's our Easter baskets! Can we get them out now?"

"It's a kaleidoscope — sort of a stained glass telescope."

"The box says this game is for kids at least seven years old, so if you play it you'll get arrested."

"The noise is keepin' us awake. Maybe some
'tato chips would help us sleep."

"It's a snow doll."

"Do I know you? I'm not allowed to talk to strangers."

"Why does Daddy take naps when he doesn't even HAVE to?"

"If you wanna see some action, go run the can opener."

"When you read my horrorscope, why does it
always say 'and be a good boy today'?"

"Are you allowed to override Mommy's veto?"

"Jeffy's drawing people with no clothes on!"

"That was very good, Dolly, but that wasn't the Pledge of Allegiance. It was a McDonald's commercial."

"But the SITTER always lets us stay up
till . . ."
"I am NOT the sitter!"

"Some of my peas got over the wall."

"Grandma? This is Billy. I can whistle!
Listen!. . ."

"The dish ran away with the spoon."

"Are you sure you're yelling at the right knob?"

"I know you won't believe it, but this beautiful young gal icing the cupcakes is really my mom."

"Wow! Daddy's watch just hums, but Grand-ma's TICKS!"

"Two's company, three's a crowd, four's too many and five's not allowed!"

"This ice cream scoop makes good snowballs."

"I know my times tables to four."
"The only times I know are my o'clocks and
half-pasts."

"How will that stuff get from down there up to my sore throat?"

"We're talkin' about old times."

"Those jets will be sorry if God catches them drawing lines on the sky."

"My zipper won't keep its teeth together."

"Look how long the jelly roll is when you
unwind it."

"I made the flag red, white and brown. I couldn't find my blue crayon."

"Hi, Charlie! I'm home!"

"I can tell you're a grandma, Mrs. Bowie,
'cause you have lots of plants."

"I've got to rememberize a poem for school."

"But, Mommy! I just took some snowballs to
bed with me last night so I could play
with them this morning."

"They're encyclopedias — in case we need to
know something and Daddy isn't here."

"Mommy, ever since you cleaned up my room,
I can't find ANYTHING!"

"Shall I get PJ's nose for you, Mommy?"

"A house of STRAW? Sounds like a real firetrap!"

"... I come from Alabama with a bandage
on my knee ..."

"Miss Helen put a steeple in there to hold my papers together."

Have Fun with the Family Circus

☐ ANY CHILDREN?	14116	$1.50
☐ CAN I HAVE A COOKIE?	14155	$1.50
☐ DADDY'S LITTLE HELPERS	14384	$1.50
☐ THE FAMILY CIRCUS	14068	$1.50
☐ FOR THIS I WENT TO COLLEGE?	14069	$1.50
☐ GOOD MORNING SUNSHINE!	14356	$1.50
☐ HELLO, GRANDMA?	14169	$1.50
☐ I CAN'T UNTIE MY SHOES	14070	$1.50
☐ I'M TAKING A NAP	14144	$1.50
☐ I NEED A HUG	14147	$1.50
☐ JEFFY'S LOOKIN' AT ME!	14096	$1.50
☐ LOOK WHO'S HERE	14207	$1.50
☐ MINE	14056	$1.50
☐ MY TURN NEXT!	14412	$1.50
☐ NOT ME!	14333	$1.50
☐ PASGHETTI AND MEAT BULBS!	14440	$1.50
☐ PEACE, MOMMY, PEACE	14145	$1.50
☐ PEEKABOO! I LOVE YOU!	14174	$1.50
☐ QUIET! MOMMY'S ASLEEP!	13930	$1.50
☐ WANNA BE SMILED AT?	14118	$1.50
☐ WHEN'S LATER, DADDY?	14124	$1.50